RADIOHEAD

GREEN PLASTIC WATERINGCAN

PHOTOGRAPHIC CREDITS

© LONDON FEATURES INTERNATIONAL LTD

© PICTORIAL PRESS

© REDFERNS

© REX PICTURES

UFO Music Ltd 18 Hanway Street London W1P 9DD England
Telephone: 0171 636 1281 Fax: 0171 636 0738

First published in Great Britain 1996
UFO Music Ltd 18 Hanway Street
London W1P 9DD

ISBN 1-873884-69-9

Designed by UFO Music Ltd

Printed by

Lawrence-Allen Ltd Weston-super-Mare Somerset

RADIOHEAD

GREEN PLASTIC WATERINGCAN

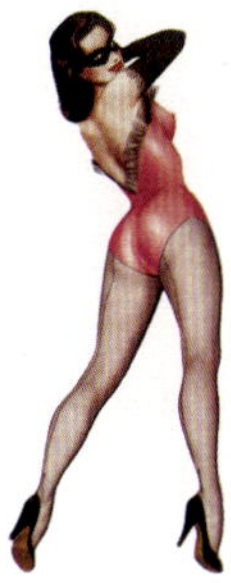

BY WILLIAM STONE

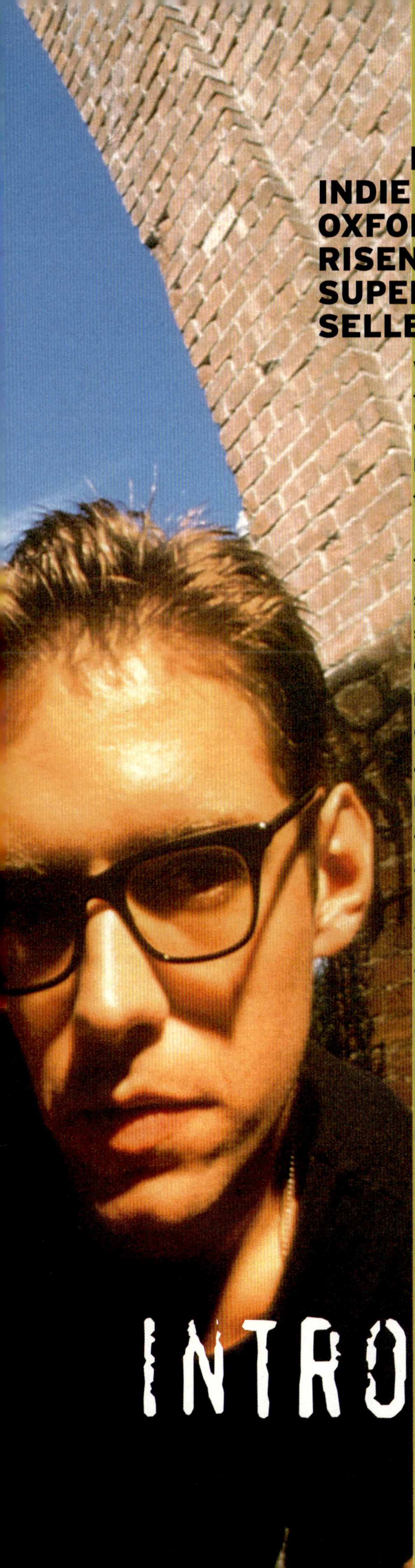

FROM THE MEAGREST OF INDIE ORIGINS IN THEIR NATIVE OXFORD, RADIOHEAD HAVE RISEN TO THE RARE STATUS OF SUPER-CREDIBLE MILLION-SELLERS. Having initially avoided damaging comparison with local shoe-gazing peers like Ride and Slowdive, they first hit big with the desolate teen anthem "Creep", a blast of noise and melody that, like Nirvana's "Smells Like Teen Spirit", aimed straight at the heart of a desperate generation.

Their debut album, "Pablo Honey" was a huge success, particularly Stateside, but it was their second, "The Bends" that hit home in the UK. Combining a big rock sound with classic songwriting, it saw singer Thom Yorke classed along with Kurt Cobain and Manic Street Preachers' Richey Edwards as an icon of alienation, Radiohead's concerts, always high points of intensity, becoming marked by an almost religious fervour with huge crowds singing along to the likes of "High and Dry" and "Iron Lung". Major tours of Europe, Japan and the US followed, Yorke in interview ever-keen to escape his newfound and unwelcome reputation.

Radiohead's most recent performances saw the introduction of numerous new songs, each clear, raucous and immensely powerful, guaranteeing the bands future domination of the charts. Nothing can stop them.

INTRODUCTION

1 ON A FRIDAY

IT'S CLAIMED INCREASINGLY OFTEN THAT, FOR BRITISH MUSIC AT LEAST,

1996 is the Year Of The Mediocre. The outrageous success of Oasis, Pulp and Blur has, it's said, created an unbreakable tyranny of style where new bands, all new bands feel forced to work within the strictest musical and lyrical parameters. Hence Britpop and the Manchester sound and their unconditional worship of The Beatles, The Kinks and the Sixties in general. Many believe Pop, Rock, whatever they care to call it this year, to be frantically treading water, if not actually floating dead.

Characters too seem in scarce supply. Where the late Eighties saw the rise of music's cult of personality, now it seems there are few left with the courage, bravado or sheer force of character to carry the torch. Even bands feted for their controversial, no-holds-barred interview techniques usually comprise of one (on rare occasions two) reasonably forthright and intriguing frontperson and a gang of faceless session-players. Most bands present their listeners/readers/ viewers with no idiosyncrasy, no real feeling, and no depth. You can't spend hours discussing the life and thoughts of each individual member or, pondering their lyrics, wonder how it was they ever found out so much about you.

The luckiest amongst them receive brief adulation from fickle fans high on novelty and out for cheap thrills. Their performances may elicit occasional explosions of teenage frenzy, with monitors draped in heaving, breathless flesh. But they have no devotees, no acolytes, no legions dedicated to the cause. Their gigs, though celebratory, fail to achieve the ecstatic heights of religious abandon found at hardcore political rallies, Billy Graham meetings, even major sporting events.

They just aren't that IMPORTANT.

Of course there were never that many bands who meant anything, whose triumphs and disasters became those of millions. Nirvana were the last. Perhaps The Cure before them. Oasis are getting there. And so, in a far quieter, almost surreptitious fashion, are Radiohead.

Formed in and around Oxford in 1986, spending some years experimenting with sounds and personnel, discovering their own strengths, Radiohead have, like all the greatest bands, never really fitted in to a scene. A rare occurrence considering how many bandwagons they might have jumped in all that time. The Baggy scene, that boisterous (some say yobbish) Northern pop/dance crossover was too frivolous for them, Britpop too lowbrow, too lightweight, too concerned with the catatonic boredom of suburban normality. Even the rather hurtfully named Shoegazing scene, which actually originated in the Oxford/Thames Valley region with the likes of Ride and Slowdive, was not enough. Periodically harsh, sometimes highly melodic, it was never fraught enough, its sudden squalls of noise seeming like temporary reawakenings from toked-out inertia rather than bursts of true emotion.

Radiohead were, are too big for that. Utterly concerned with their own sound, problems and potential, they're too bloody-minded, too damn stubborn to suffer easy categorisation. As any scene-members, even the prime movers eventually discover to their own immense discomfort, they either stand on their own or not at all.

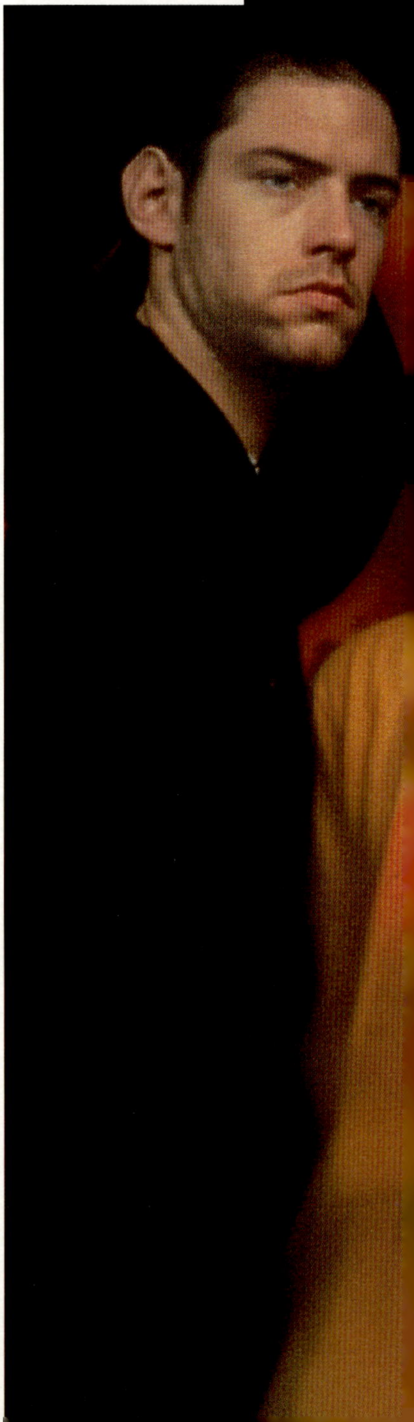

ON A FRIDAY

2 PROVE YOURSELF

THOM YORKE WAS BORN IN WELLINGBOROUGH, NORTHAMPTONSHIRE ON OCTOBER 7TH, 1968, soon relocating to Scotland due to his father's job as a purveyor of equipment in the chemical engineering industry. North of the border, Yorke's home was by the sea, specifically near a beach still guarded by bunkers and wrapped in barbed wire from World War II (though this is unlikely to have contributed to Yorke's later insecurities). Thom remembers his father, a champion pugilist at university, one day presenting him with a pair of boxing gloves and attempting to teach him the in-and-outs of that most gentlemanly of sports. He no doubt thought that Thom, even now only five foot five and pencil-thin, would benefit from a crash-course in self-defence. With hindsight, he could certainly have done without being consistently decked by his dad.

But size, or lack of it, was not Yorke's major concern - that, unfortunately, was right in his face every time he looked in a mirror. Born with one eye closed and paralysed, he underwent five serious operations before reaching the tender age of six and was forced to wear an eyepatch for a full year. Muscle grafts, that kind of thing. Rather than receiving tributes from the other kids for his buccaneering appearance, he was nicknamed Salamander and teased mercilessly. With every change of school or area came a new set of derogatory monikers and yet more bullying and abuse. Fights were commonplace, victories less so. It's taken Yorke years to even approach coming to terms with this facial oddity. Even now he mentions an occasion when, while working in a bar aged eighteen, he was told by some woman that his eyes were beautiful but completely wrong.

By the time he was eight, his family had moved to Oxford, his homebase to this present day. By twelve he was at Abingdon, a minor public school on the outskirts of town. Yorke hated it with a vengeance, considering it less a seat of learning than a fully-fledged ducking-stool. He did though forge a friendship with another bona fide child of Camus, Colin Greenwood. Gatecrashing the same house parties, the pair - Greenwood decked out in bodystocking and beret, Yorke in lipstick, mascara and oversized dinner jacket - would eschew flirtation and revelry in favour of hijacking the stereo-system and replacing the turbo-charged dance music with a caustic melange of Magazine and Joy Division.

Their deviant appearance must surely have saved them from many more beatings than they actually received (beatings apparently administered by friends of Philip Selway, one year older and later Radiohead's drummer).

Having been given a Spanish guitar for his eighth birthday, Yorke was already keen to form a band. He drifted into a school punk outfit but, given his musical heroes, stiff-wristed thrashing was never going to satisfy. Greenwood seemed more of a soulmate so the two, with Greenwood on bass, began tossing ideas about and seeing what stuck. Soon Selway came onboard, then on guitar Ed O'Brien, an impossibly tall Hugh Grant lookalike (though at the time he more resembled Morrissey) that Colin met during a school stage production of Gilbert & Sullivan's 'Trial By Jury'.

Convincing the local vicar that they were a serious jazz combo, they were permitted to rehearse in a nearby church hall. Greenwood's brother Jonny, three years younger than the others and a viola player for the Thames Vale Youth Orchestra, would hang around and, more often than not, ask to join in. Eventually, beginning as the harmonica player, then moving via keyboards to guitar, he became a fulltime member. Practising on Fridays, they called themselves, not entirely unreasonably, On A Friday.

Soon college became a distraction and, leaving Greenwood Minor to his own devices, they all went their separate ways. Ed O'Brien took off to Manchester University, Selway to Liverpool Polytechnic (where he at one point played drums in a production of C. S Lewis' 'Return to the Forbidden Planet'). Colin Greenwood went up to Cambridge, actually Peterhouse College, where he rose to the lofty position of Entertainments Officer. Exhibiting taste of rare ecleticism, he put on shows by Humphrey Littleton, the James Taylor Quartet and, suspiciously often, himself. Yorke left his job in a menswear department (he's still known to rant on about his loathed boss, and toy with the idea of driving large vehicles very quickly through the shop-front) to study Fine Art and Literature at Exeter University and dabbled in sampler technology while playing guitar for an electro-ensemble called Flickernoise. Yorke's artwork, heavily influenced by Francis Bacon, was never really considered up to scratch, even his own favourite composition, that of a man blowing his own head off. It was only when computers were introduced that he could truly come into his own. A self-proclaimed Ideas Man, he'd scan in 16th Century Italian paintings (on one occasion the whole of the Sistine Chapel) and fuck about, colouring, twisting and smudging until something new was born. It may not have been Fine Art in the strictest sense, but it got him a degree.

RADIOHEAD **GREEN PLASTIC WATERINGCAN**

During vacations, On A Friday continued to write and rehearse, occasionally playing out at the low-key likes of Oxford's Jericho Tavern and the Rock Garden in Covent Garden (doubtless, in years to come, that particular gig will rival The Sex Pistols at the 100 Club for the number of thousands who claim to have attended. Since the tabloids are unlikely to have missed out on an example of mass asphyxiation to match the Black Hole Of Calcutta, we can rest assured they'll all be lying). With the sound as yet not settled upon, the band sometimes found themselves struggling with bizarre circumstances, not least when they attempted to include a wind section consisting of three saxophones.

Gradually all other peripheral members were phased out, Yorke and the other four finding it harder and harder to write parts to suit. It wasn't that they were betraying their more radical roots (Howard Devoto and Magazine were seldom lambasted for lacking musical flamboyance and adventurism), simply that the band had discovered that one of their greatest strengths lay in their songwriting - their clear, uncomplicated, popsong writing.

'I know the reason we're here,' said Yorke later, as Radiohead began their final push towards the real big time. *'because, in one guise or another, we've always written screaming pop songs. We were always aware that any one of our songs goes so much further than other people's. We've always been aware of just being a pop band. But that's because of the way we write and the way we perform. It happened by accident. We didn't intend to be in a pop band, we just happened to be in one.'*

Meanwhile, the band's first reviews began to appear around the Oxford area, most of which were hugely enthusiastic despite being utterly unable to pin On A Friday down to any specific genre or scene (funny that). One live-piece on a gig at the Jericho Tavern contained a veritable stampede of disparate references - REM, Madchester, Country & Western, even Kirk Brandon from The Pack, Theatre Of Hate and Spear Of Destiny. What came across mostly though was how impressed these people were with the band's attitude, their narrow-eyed unwillingness to play it straight, follow the crowd, take the easy option. Yorke's voice came in for special commendation, close to embarrassingly in a review of a two-track demo containing 'Stop Whispering' and 'What Is That You Say'

It was time to get serious.

Demos were selling, glowing reviews were there for the taking. On A Friday moved into a house together in Oxford, presumably assuming close proximity would be an aid to creativity, and the individual members sought gainful employment (even the cheapest equipment is pie in the sky to dole boys). Selway tried teaching English Language as well as undergoing a stint in Publishing as a Desk Editor. O'Brien had a go at assisting a photographer and, like Yorke, worked bars. Colin Greenwood, for his sins, ended up behind the counter in Our Price where staff were cruelly forcefed the hits of the day and, from time to time, bodysearched on the way out, lest they escape with expensive and hard-to-find twelve-inch imports concealed in their Y-fronts.

The house-sharing project rapidly came to grief.

If cleanliness is next to Godliness then Radiohead went to the Devil at breathtaking pace. This was grime time, the place resembling Munster Mansion after a Young Ones residency and a grenade assault from Mossad. Soon only Colin Greenwood remained, along with Yorke who now spent his time at home, threatening the foundations with forms of techno unlikely to soundtrack any Summer Of Love. In fact, Yorke had problems with a lot of the dance music prevalent in those years.

However, career movement was afoot with the band receiving a call from two young fellows named Chris Hufford and Bryce Edge. Ex-members of a, gulp, New Romantic band called Aeriel FX - they may or may not have once supported Spandau Ballet, it's very hard to care - these two had set up their own management company. All they needed was a band to make their name. On A Friday seemed like the one. Agreements were struck and things became just that little bit better co-ordinated.

'It was a period of acute embarrassment,' he explains. 'I kept trying to go to raves and stuff. Then I thought 'Fuck this, I'm not standing in a field getting the fear at five in the morning'. I understand some of the music, I was pretty into it at college. But I couldn't afford any synthesisers and it wasn't the stuff I'd grown up on. It just didn't have the same emotional appeal.'

The gigging continued, and the writing and rehearsing. Confidence grew at monstrous pace, to the point where the sending out of demos became more than a mere tossing of tapes into postal oblivion. Replies were expected. And received. Big time. In mid-1991, On A Friday's final concert (they only ever played eight or so) ended in chaos with between fifteen and twenty A&R men howling for tequila, cocaine and signatures on the dotted line, if you please. Hufford and Edge - the latter being no relation to Damon, the genius singer/sonic engineer with Chrome who was found only after having lain dead in his flat for over a month in late 1995 - had come up trumps, and continued to do so, setting the major labels off against each other, seeking the very best of deals.

The winners? PARLOPHONE!!!

Now, under some considerable pressure from the company, the band came to realise their dire need for a change of name. On A Friday may appear all well and good when knocking out a few tunes for friends and relatives of a weekend but, out in the real world, it's better suited to a warm-up act for The Village People. Radiohead, taken from the title of a track on Talking Heads 'True Stories', seemed like a cool one. Plus, the band had been given exactly two weeks to come up with something and, with two hours to go Talking Heads was what was on the stereo. Sometimes fate is known to lend a hand. Besides, everyone knows that bands and songs with Radio in their name always get more airtime than anyone else. It's a mutual respect thing, nominal nepotism. Or so it's reckoned.

3 cREEP

THE RELATIONSHIP WITH PARLOPHONE WAS IMMEDIATELY PROBLEMATIC, THE BAND'S INTEGRITY BEING CALLED INTO QUESTION. Integrity is a word that springs up often when people are on the subject of Important Bands, Integrity and its bosom buddy Honesty. Honesty, a facade of honesty, or at least an honest facade are things that allow people to relate to a band's work, to feel that they are not being tricked and lied to, as they feel they are by everyone else. Some see the struggle of bands to avoid losing their honesty, their integrity, their souls in the heart of the corporate machine as being one of the great spectator sports of the late Twentieth Century. Some, Clash or Nirvana fans for instance, have long considered it much more important than that.

Radiohead had to make a decision. Would they release their records on Parlophone straight and risk accusations of being nothing more than capitalist whores, flogging teenage angst from flats the size of Kensington Palace? Or would they release through some new label set up by the major to fake indie credibility? To their eternal credit they said it like it was - major they were, major they would be. And anyway they liked the contract they'd signed, tying them to Parlophone in all territories, throughout the Universe, known and unknown. Yorke in particular appreciated the breadth of vision and ambition inherent in the deal. BUT, INDIE OR MAJOR, AT THIS TIME THEY WERE STILL NOTHING.

They had no clear idea of their own sound, of how they might consider themselves, just a set of songs written at different times, in different places, in different moods over the last five or so years. In the parlance of 1996, they remained invalid, invalidated, whatever.

They took to the road for their first concerted effort at a tour and almost straight away began to lose whatever it was they had in the first place. Yorke hacked off his hair, reducing it to the most violent of crewcuts, lending his appearance a quality of seriously spiky aggression he hoped would help drive the music on to ever-greater heights of intensity. He smoked too much, drank way too much, gigs were cancelled. He had to calm down.

Shows were arranged with an alarming variety of acts, some good, some bad, some abysmal beyond hope of recall. They supported Kingmaker (not good gigs these, no opportunity to soundcheck), The Sultans Of Ping FC, The Frank and Walters, Spiritualized, even cabaret types like Doctor and The Medics, taking any chance offered to learn something new, hone their sound, perfect those songs.

Finally they enter the studio at Chipping Norton with Sean Slade and Paul Q Kolderie and a pattern of work begins to emerge. Yorke arrives with chord changes and vocal harmonies, the very bones of a few songs. Jonny Greenwood adds guitar, maybe some extra sounds, brief bursts of eye-bulging distortion that could never be accurately described as solos, perhaps some extra half-melodies. Then the band arrange it together, carve a song from the singular mess.

The first results were included on the 'Drill' EP, released in May 1992. The main track, 'Prove Yourself' was the clearest of pointers to what was to come, with Yorke crooning the extraordinarily morbid line 'I'm better off dead' while Greenwood hammered chords through his pedals, making his guitar sound like the grunting of a dying elephant. Above all, 'Prove Yourself' was a scintillating SONG, like the best of early U2 minus the bomblast and overbearing megalomania. In blackhearted mockery of the band's name, it got no airplay at all, eventually charting at a pleasingly significant 101.

Radiohead continued to tour, by the end of the year playing over a hundred shows - amazing for a band without a sniff at even an indie hit. They also released a follow-up single, another EP A-sided by the song that would eventually make their fortune, seal their reputation and, to a large degree, blight their lives. A steady relationship since his college days had not lessened Yorke's unbelievable capacity for self-loathing. Even when togged up to the nines, preening and posing along with Colin Greenwood at parties, any sense of arrogance or superiority (an eternal must for the heroic outsider) was wholly undermined by his lack of faith in himself and his looks. Years of piss-taking and humiliation are bound to take their toll, particularly when people are taking the piss on grounds over which you have absolutely no control. And though Yorke was later to claim that the lipstick and mascara were simply signs of his learning to live life FOR EFFECT, that he'd change records over FOR EFFECT, get on the bus FOR EFFECT, and that his years at college were the first he'd spent among people who also lived it large, who also realised the importance of looks, his lyrics have always betrayed a critical lack of self-confidence in that area.

'Creep' saw Yorke slicing himself open with a surgeon's precision. The concept was simple. One person, any person feeling ugly or stupid or simply ordinary looks at their bright, glamourous, unattainable object of desire and feels worse, feels bitter, feels small, and perhaps even finds power in the hopelessness of it all. The oft-quoted chorus pretty much says it all - 'I wish I was special/You're so fucking special/But I'm a creep/I'm a weirdo/What the hell am I doing here?

Later, in Hits Magazine, Yorke would describe the song like this: *"'Creep' is more the way people look at you. The guy in the song doesn't necessarily believe that he's a creep, but he's being told he is. But these things change. 'Creep' is the term for someone who follows people around and drinks on his own in bars and stuff, but the idea came from a rocky relationship I was having.'*

'I find it very disturbing that there are thousands and thousands of these wonderful love songs which aren't really wonderful at all, and it's evident that the people who were writing them have never even been close to anything resembling the emotions they represent. Love songs have been killed by mainstream music, and to actually write a love song is a kind of peculiar thing to do these days.'

Unlike 'Prove Yourself', 'Creep' was backed by music of rare power, where a tinkling guitar suddenly detonates into quite awestriking violence. This was a rock epic direct from the old school, complete with the clinical timing of, say, Judas Priest's 'Beyond The Realms Of Death'. Two things saved it from becoming such a melodramatic gross-out though. First Thom's tiny, broken voice as he faces the enormity of his own physical misfortune, a voice finally soaring to peaks of almost ecstatic acceptance. And then Jonny Greenwood's guitar, specifically that now-notorious chopping effect immediately before Yorke's vocal explosion. **It's a perfect moment, an inimitably filthy noise even Kurt Cobain might have been proud to inflict upon his audience.**

Various stories are told explaining how this infernal, beautiful interruption came about.

It depends which band member is talking. Greenwood himself has claimed that it was merely the product of his doing his job. He didn't particularly like the song, apparently, thought it too simple, possibly even a little wimpy. It just needed beefing up with a few extra points of interest and that is always where he comes in. Others have reckoned it was a sound Greenwood often made when checking to see if his guitar was loud enough, or distorted enough, or even on at all, and the band decided to utilise it to greater effect. Or it might have been pure accident, something Slade and Kolderie picked up on during one unusually experimental jamming session and committed to tape. Whatever the truth of it (and these things are often best left as the stuff of mythology), it was one heavy, heavy monster sound which contributed massively to a song that set Radiohead far outside the norm.

Strangely for such a melodic powerhouse of a record and despite a fair amount of press (not all good, it must be said), 'Creep' only made it to Number 72 in the charts. It was deemed too depressing for radio, even with the kind of financial backing that ordinarily puts a smile on everyone's face.

The touring continued relentlessly, Radiohead now playing to ridiculously enthusiastic crowds of around three hundred. And, in October 1992, approximately one year into their major deal, they put together their debut album, a process that took no longer than three weeks.

The year ended on a high note. 'Creep' was named in the Top Ten singles by the New Musical Express and was found to have sold in excess of 12,000 copies. It had also begun to go down an absolute storm live. With the album and a new single ready to go, 1993 could only be better. How much better no one could have predicted.

4 ANYONE CAN PLAY GUITAR

IT STARTED SLOWLY BUT HUGELY CONVINCINGLY.

Radiohead were picked out by both Melody Maker and the New Musical Express as a band to watch out for in 1993. Mind you, this is no guarantee of success, or even of getting a one-page interview.

More importantly, the band went out on their debut headlining tour and, though the venues were still on the small side, were greeted by audiences better described as riotous assemblies. Tickets were changing hands at £35 a shot, more than twice what you'd have coughed up to see Prince's dead sexy two-part extravaganza at Wembley Arena. Melody Maker caught up with them at their second show and, with typically dour decorum, declared them to be 'perfect'. They also awarded 'Anyone Can Play Guitar', Radiohead's third single, the accolade of Single Of The Week, as did the infinitely more sober Music Week.

'Anyone Can Play Guitar' seemed a strange release after 'Creep'. It was way more upbeat lyrically and possessed of Radiohead's usual tunefulness, but somehow it seemed TOO melodic, like a composite of classic tracks, each one vaguely, even irritatingly familiar. In this way it was probably three years ahead of its time. Their fans liked it though, and they quite clearly all bought it in the first week of release because, without a single play on day-time radio, it jumped the charts at Number 32 then fell straight back out again. A warning to all up and coming hopefuls in the crazy world of rock and roll: never, ever put the word Radio in your band name or the titles of your songs. You won't get played. It's a jealousy thing, you see, a nominal negativity. Believe it - **if they wouldn't play 'Creep' or 'Anyone Can Play Guitar' you haven't got a hope in hell.**

Three weeks later 'Pablo Honey', that debut LP, its name taken from one of the beastlier tracks by America's legendary hoax-callers The Jerky Boys (Radiohead had borrowed the tape from Chapterhouse) went into the UK album charts at Number 20. Essentially a cobbled together affair made up of the three singles, some B-sides and a few new tracks, it was nonetheless treated with great respect by most critics.

The lyrics, as would always be the case after one listen to 'Creep' and a single experience watching Radiohead's fanatical fans sing every word to every song, came in for particular scrutiny. and some interesting points were raised. Yorke, it was said, was struggling against two separate cliches. The first was that the British are emotionally and sexually repressed beyond all reason, cracking finally and for all time only under the most extreme duress. This might explain Yorke's own use of cliches like 'You are the sun and the moon and the stars are you' (cliche often being the language of those who would really rather not express themselves), and it might explain why, on tracks like 'Ripcord', 'Vegetable' and, of course 'Creep' he sounded so wracked, stretched and torn to pieces by his own ultimately irrepressible feelings. And the other cliche was, quite naturally, that boys don't cry. Yorke is the type to dig within himself, weep deep puddles of pure anguish, then kick you in the balls and drown you in them, just for daring to tell him what he can and cannot be.

Boys don't cry? Get this, you WANKER.

Up until May, the touring was more or less constant. Then a new single, 'Pop Is Dead' came out. Where its predecessor 'Anyone Can Play Guitar', with its lyrics apparently sarcastically shadowing Jim Morrisson's 'I got my eyes on the road and my hands up on the whee-eel' seemed a blast against the hoary iconography of rock (some said Yorke was simply jealous because his girlfriend claimed to fancy the long-dead Lizard King), 'Pop Is Dead' was a far harsher statement. **Yorke firmly believed that young talent was being strangled in the UK,** that the business, being a business was not looking to take risks, that the press was not out there digging furiously for new acts and that radio, well, fuck radio.

Given that many of his favourite Oxford contemporaries were clearly slipping through the net, that the music press were increasingly prone to fatuous categorisation, and that the business was indeed a business, he undoubtedly had a point. The crunch came though with the reviews received by 'Pop Is Dead', in the national press they were far from euphoric. Even some of the live reviews from Spring 1993 felt like the knotted end of a backlash. U2 comparisons began to abound, the gigs were held up as festivals of easy-to-swallow angst for prepubescents. It wasn't very nice (This was not true of the noble members of the regional press, mind you. Well aware of the effect Radiohead's guerrilla raids had on their local gig-goers, some of them actually banded together and petitioned Radio One for extra airplay for Radiohead).

Thom Yorke, extremely sensitive at the best of times, found the criticism hard to deal with. The out-and-out abuse was harder. A dyed-in-the-wool music fan, even something of a buff, he was given to spending his Wednesdays perusing the inkie press. Before, it had occasionally pissed him off. Now, after reading someone describe Radiohead as 'a lily-livered excuse for a rock band', it took him a week to recover. To make things worse, 'Pop Is Dead' entered the charts at Number 42 and promptly fell away. All momentum in the band's career appeared to have been lost. Yorke's confidence, hardly at bursting point anyway, was severely deflated. Radiohead left to tour Europe and then the States, hoping against hope that something, somewhere would turn things around.

5 PABLO HONEY

IN FACT, THE FIRST MAJOR TURNAROUND IN RADIOHEAD'S SHORT CAREER WAS ALREADY TAKING PLACE

- in Israel, a traditional venue for First Comings. Apparently some DJ rather took a shine to 'Creep', span it regularly, sent out a few shouts of big respect to the Oxford Massive and caused enough ructions for the rest of his peers to want a piece of this Brit action too. 'Creep', for no real reason other than it was an especially fine song, went straight into the Israeli Top Ten.

Of course, this was hardly big news, no cause to be bathing in Moet Chandon or emptying those Colt 45's into the ceiling. Every band is big somewhere. Take the case of Powder - big in Japan even though they were quite evidently not even the best band in their own house.

But then more news started coming in, bigger news, better news. 'Creep' had hit in New Zealand. Then it was Spain. Then Scandinavia. Then finally, unbelievably America.

Initially available only on import, 'Creep' was played only by very few radio stations. The response from the public though took even DJs well accustomed to overkill completely by surprise. Linked to their listeners by 24-hour request lines (hey, we're your buddies, feel free to call us anytime), they soon had to leave the phones off the hook. It was blindingly apparent what everyone seemed to want to hear... over and over and over again. College radio, that consummate breaker of 'alternative' acts Stateside took up the torch (a brilliant term, 'alternative', so shamelessly meaningless). Soon KROQ in Los Angeles, which claims rather boastfully to be the most influential station on the planet, had 'Creep' at Number One on its playlist. It was only a matter of time before MTV had the video on heavy, heavy monster rotation, where it remained throughout a long, hot and increasingly Creepy summer.

Radiohead's problems in Britain suddenly seemed a very long way away, even further than those unarguable five thousand miles. Having completed the European leg of their tour, it had begun to dawn on them that something big and potentially rather scary was afoot. In June they touched down on American ground to find that Capitol (the US equivalent of Parlophone) had responded to burgeoning public demand by rush-releasing 'Pablo Honey' and setting their nationwide sales forces on Red Alert (it's British music, captain, but not as we know it). A huge campaign was organised and Radiohead, who'd turned down a series of extremely prestigious support slots on major tours, took to the road on a headline club trip, faced with crowd reactions that, had they not seemed so incredibly weird, would have scared the shit out of them. Many of the gigs had sold out before the band had even left continental Europe, the Whiskey on Los Angeles Sunset Boulevard (opposite Johnny Depp's Viper Rooms, gorehounds) doing so in twenty minutes flat.

The tour became a rollercoaster ride of terrifying proportions. After meeting and greeting salespeople, record shop owners, distributors, CD packers, press officers, journalists, promoters, security guards, cameramen, lighting crews, DJs, VJs, conceivably even the O'Jays, Radiohead became uncomfortably conscious of exactly how many hands there are in the United States Of America. Repetitive Strain Injuries were not out of the question. The idea that 'Pablo Honey' had also sold 50,000 copies in Canada must have been a very real cause for concern.

Back in Britain, the press began to cotton on,

London's Evening Standard even running an article entitled 'British Pop Unknowns Storm USA'. Now the storming of the USA by British bands is not an unknown occurrence. Remember The Beatles, The Rolling Stones and The Kinks? Elton John, David Bowie, T.Rex and Gary Glitter (actually, maybe The Leader missed out)? Duran Duran and Culture Club? More recently the USA had even been stormed by EMF and Jesus Jones, though you can't help but feel that's more like being infested with rats. No, 'The British are coming' is a well-worn phrase in America, as is 'The new British Chart Invasion'. Nevertheless, on this side of the pond we do tend to get carried away by the idea. Maybe it's a reaction to Coca-Cola, McDonalds and American cultural imperialism, maybe it's to do with a pulsing race memory of the War Of Independence but we do like to see Our Chaps stick one up Johnny Yank. And in Radiohead's case, where a band more or less rejected in their own country were slaying them bigtime, well, something had to be done. Radiohead were definitely up for re-adoption.

The inkies, who had, to be honest and despite Yorke's claims to the contrary, been more than supportive, pricked up their ears.

Steve Wright read out the Evening Standard article on his Radio One afternoon show. The seeds sown by 'Pablo Honey' and the first three singles had well and truly ripened. Radiohead's British harvest festival approached.

Meanwhile in the USA the madness continued, now under the official banner of HEADMANIA.

With the tour sold out, all they could do was extend. 'Creep' spent a month in the mainstream singles charts making them the first 'new' British band to break into the American Top Forty since the KLF, 'Pablo Honey' sold upwards of half a million copies. Radiohead were invited onto the vastly popular Arsenio Hall TV Show and even had one understandably frantic live show broadcast on television. It was quite clear that they could do no wrong.

Now Parlophone Britain had a thought - it basically went like this. Oi, if the Yanks are having it, why not our lot? The idea was mooted to re-release 'Creep'. After all, if it could become an anthem for the lost, alienated or even mildly sulky youth of America, surely the British would catch on. They'd gone for Nirvana. Initially the band themselves were not keen. They were still obviously young and hungry not simply for success. A further chance to test themselves in the studio might have been nice. Moving on was always their way. Nevertheless the record company managed to persuade them otherwise, and producers Slade and Kolderie helped sway them. 'Creep', they reckoned, was a magnificent track. They should give more people a chance to hear it. In fact, the way things were going, everyone was going to get a chance to hear it.

So 'Creep' it was.

This time radio was up for it. The song went to Number Seven in the UK singles chart and stayed in the Top Twenty for a month. Popping back to Blighty to celebrate this overdue success and to play Reading (an appearance eventually cancelled when Yorke's throat seized up through advanced stress), Radiohead remained only briefly. A further American tour had been arranged for them, this time supporting Belly whose 'Star' LP was soon to become a million-seller. This was a real treat for the band. Not only did they get on fabulously with the headliners but they also cited Tanya Donelly, from her days in Throwing Muses, as one of their greatest influences (Slade and Kolderie had actually been chosen as producers for 'Pablo Honey' because of their Throwing Muses connections). Yorke and Donelly would finish every show with a duet of Belly's 'Untogether'.

From the States it was on to Canada and a support slot with the impossibly bombastic Tears For Fears.

Horrible though it must have been, it did introduce them to a new audience, as well as allowing them to play to those who'd sent 'Pablo Honey' platinum in that country. It should come as no surprise whatsoever to anyone at all that, once Radiohead had gone their own merry way, Tears For Fears' Roland Orzabal chose to perform his own singular version of 'Creep'. (Chrissie Hynde has also since covered it, and it made an appearance on the soundtrack to Steven Dorff's painfully fraught movie 'SFW' - SFW as in So Fucking What).

Radiohead's return to their own country was nothing short of triumphant. Playing December shows in Europe and the UK with James (one band who'd survived an almighty critical kicking) they sold out all shows and received almost embarrassing plaudits from all comers. Come Christmas Poll time, they blew away the opposition. 'Creep' was Number Four on Billboard's Modern Rock Tracks of 1993, Number One with writers for Rolling Stone, Number Two in Melody Maker. Readers Polls were even more positive. Number One in Melody Maker and the New Musical Express, tied with Suede's 'Animal Nitrate' in Select, only just pipped by Take that's 'Pray' when Radio One's listeners voted for the Brit Awards. Perhaps even more impressively, it was ranked at Number Thirty-Nine in Radio One's Top One Hundred Songs Of All Time. This was acclaim bordering on adulation.

After 120 gigs played and untold thousands of miles travelled, 1993 had turned out to be a pretty good year.

6 BLOW OUT

A PRETTY GOOD YEAR? WELL, IT CERTAINLY APPEARED THAT WAY FROM THE OUTSIDE.

Within Camp Radiohead a starkly different attitude ruled, any outstanding pairs of rose-tinted spectacles having been crushed to dust and twisted metal under the wheels of the tour bus that had driven them remorselessly back and forth across America.

The problems had really started on the second leg of that seemingly endless American jaunt, just after 'Creep' had finally hit big in the UK, Parlophone had pressed the Belly Button and Radiohead found themselves back out on the road. It wasn't really that they'd grown to hate each other, though that would have been easily understandable after two years cooped up in vans, buses and dressing-rooms. With members as affable and polite as O'Brien and as idiosyncratic and entertaining as the Greenwoods (a pair most certainly not from the Gallagher school of brotherhood) that could never happen. It was more because they'd seen all the movies, read all the books and magazines, played all the card-games, conquered the Gameboys, tried the food, the wine and the spirits, collected the air-miles and generally drunk deep from what they'd always assumed to be the cup of plenty. Beyond that, way beyond that, they'd been playing the same songs for two whole years, the same old thing in hundreds of different places. Stasis had set in. They'd basically stopped communicating, both onstage and off.

Yorke, of course, had reacted much worse than the others. It was he, after all, who was endlessly referred to as The 'Creep' Guy. HE had to fend off the remorseless, abrasive barrage of questions, always the same fucking questions. HE had to relive the moments, try to re-enact the horror on a nightly basis. And HE had to come up with another set of songs pretty damn sharpish because 'Creep' wouldn't carry them forever. In fact, at that time 'Creep' felt less like an achievement than a cheesewire round the neck slowly, slowly drawing tighter. Yorke, the only one amongst them who genuinely preferred working in the studio to live performance, had more than had his fill of THIS lark.

BUT WORSE, MUCH, MUCH WORSE,

like countless others before him and a multitude yet to come, Thom Yorke began to disappear up his own arsehole. Life on the road can be wholly displacing, particularly on your first tour of the Big Country and especially when that tour is continually extended. Add to this a sudden, unexpected and merciless wave of acclaim (they may be crap at rowing but, when it comes to sycophancy, the Americans take gold without breaking sweat) and you're onto a real mindblower. Yorke, revealing the arrogant side to his nature that was always coupled with the wincing, brutalised aspect (think 'Creep', think newfound, exceptionally well-buffed confidence), began to believe the hype. He felt he was the top dog, the one with the true, uncompromising vision of pain and beauty, the be-all and end-all of Radiohead. Who exactly did he need? He even came up with the idea of splitting the band and going it alone.

To be a proper musician, he reasoned, a full-blown tortured artist, you HAD to be alone.

A person needs time and space to really concentrate on the incomprehensible scale of their own misfortune. Musically and, to an extent personally, he approached Spike Milligan's famous description of the late and very great Tony Hancock

'One by one he shut the door on all the people he knew; then he shut the door on himself'.

The crisis point was reached at the start of the European dates with James. Every single member of the band would much rather have been at home. Except Yorke who was plagued by the deep suspicion that, so changed must he be by the American experience, he would no longer be welcome.

A meeting was called. Yorke gave full voice to his difficulties and fears, the others vented their own feelings and it soon became clear that the weirdness and ill communication had not gone on long enough to cause any real gripes or grudges. Besides, they were still friends, had been for years, and what was the point in breaking up a band after only one album? Surely 'Pablo Honey' was only the tip of the iceberg. They needed to work hard to achieve their potential and, hopefully, at the same time blow 'Creep' right out of the water.

With all this out in the open, the shows were as exhilarating for the band as they were for the enraptured audiences.

Radiohead were BACK.

At least they thought they were. The beginning of 1994 saw them enter the studio with a bunch of new songs. Well, not actually that new, many of them having been conceived immediately after the recording of 'Pablo Honey'. But where 'Pablo Honey' had been raced through in a matter of weeks, this time there was to be no easy passage.

Maybe the pressure of having to follow up such a barnstorming success held them back, maybe the whole recording situation was just too unfamiliar after such a long period away, maybe they needed extra time to rediscover the internal band dynamic they'd left out on Highway 1000.

Perhaps it was even that success did them no favours, that they worked best when it was them against the world and having the world on their side gave them nothing to struggle against. Whatever the reason, Jonny Greenwood describes the sessions like this:

'We were playing like paranoid little mice in cages. We were scared of our instruments, scared of every note not being right.'

Nevertheless, aside from the material they DID actually manage to lay down, the time in the studio had one positive result in that it gave the band a chance to hear the songs again and think about arrangements. It also allowed them, during February, March and April, to begin forging a relationship with John Leckie, their chosen producer for the project. Though for many outside the band he'd been picked purely for his outrageous success with the first Stone Roses LP, the reality was quite different. Radiohead, and first and foremost Yorke and Colin Greenwood, were harking back to their halcyon days in Oxford, back before the band had ever started. They were looking for the John Leckie who'd worked on Magazine's art-punk classic 'Real Life'.

There was insufficient time to record an album anyway, and certainly not an album that would state once and for all that Radiohead were one of the world's greatest bands and not just That Creep Guy and his four faceless friends. A world tour had been organised, a proper world tour, not another stultifying million mile trek around the States. This was The Big One. Spain and Italy saw superb shows before capacity crowds. Three dates in the UK culminated in a show at the Astoria that TNT Magazine described with entirely commendable exuberance thus:

'Radiohead emerged to shrieks and squeals and the odd cry of 'WE LOVE YOU, THOM!' We love you, Thom? This isn't bloody Take That! Then the penny dropped. What I was watching was a coronation. Radiohead are next in line for the throne. Go away and die, U2. Abdicate, James. Radiohead are the new kings of stadium rock'.

In all the furore, no one seemed to notice that Yorke was suffering from fractured ankles. It's even difficult to tell now when you watch the video of that London show, released in March 1995 under the uniquely compelling title '27.5.94. The Astoria London Live'.

Back to the tour. Switzerland, Germany, then Japan, Hong Kong (MTV Asia giving them more air time than any 'alternative' rock band before them - oops, that WORD again), Australia and New Zealand, with a killer performance at Glastonbury thrown in for good measure. The album was all but completed with John Leckie during a brief break in June. Soon after this, calls and faxes began to arrive from the Mean Fiddler Organisation requesting that everyone treat Yorke's throat with due care and attention. It worked - Radiohead finally played the increasingly well-conceived Reading Festival.

The gigs were going well, the band were getting to see the world and not just the dusty environs of Wheres that, Idaho.

But what everyone desperately wanted to hear were some new tunes.

7 IRON LUNG

IT DIDN'T QUITE HAPPEN THE WAY EVERYBODY EXPECTED.

After all the touring, all the gladhanding (Yorke called it 'Sucking Satan's cock'), after the incredible sales figures achieved by 'Pablo Honey' and THAT SINGLE, the world and its mother thought Radiohead couldn't fail to go ballistic. But their first new single in an age, 'My Iron Lung' - released in September 1994 - was not actually that well received. Yorke had begun writing it on the morning he'd failed to turn up at Reading Festival. Later he'd remembered a picture he'd ceaselessly worked with at art college, a picture of a child with his head protruding from some metallic Fifties breathing apparatus. This gave him his lyrics, and a chance to take a pot-shot at what he thought Radiohead had become, a band broken by the business yet kept going in a sickening form of half-life by the thing they most despised - 'Creep'.

Radio One (oh no, surely not) deemed it 'too raucous', possibly because, after various attempts to perfect it in the studio, the band had finally stumbled upon the perfect take live in London in August. Reviews were fairly tepid and, though hugeness was predicted, the single only went Top Thirty. Colin Greenwood later came up with a theory to explain it, saying that the band had entered the studio that February with the clear intention of laying down a couple of sure-fire singles, true album tracks to be dealt with later. That extra pressure may well have contributed to their initial difficulties. Radiohead, he thought, might have done better to have completed the LP and chosen the singles to be taken from it later.

But eventually the muted reaction didn't matter, if anything it made the band fight harder, took them back to the good old bad old days when their backs were up against the wall and they really felt like they had something to prove. Yorke has always aimed that one of his prime motivations is his uncontrollable desire to rub critics' faces in the shit they've thrown at him. Whatever doesn't kill him, as the saying goes, only serves to make him stronger.

Radiohead kept their cool and continued their concerted assault on the rest of the world, ending up with major shows in both Thailand and Mexico. Of course, they also found time to service their ever-loyal British fans, playing a series of shows in the Autumn that took them, as per usual, back to Yorke's old college town of Exeter and back to the Old Gaol in Abingdon where they raised £37,000 for the Oxfam Rwanda Appeal. They also, along with Pulp, Ride, Supergrass, St Etienne and Neneh Cherry, involved themselves in a campaign to save Oxford's Jericho Tavern from being gutted and transformed into a £3,250,000 theme pub. Thom Yorke clearly stated his complete dismay at the idea, saying that Radiohead would never have got started without the venue.

Meanwhile, rumours abounded that Radiohead's second album, due for release in February and apparently going under the working title of 'Mint' (was it guaranteed to make loads of money? serve as the perfect accompaniment to 'The Lamb Lies down On Broadway? who knew?) would be the best rock album of 1995.

There was nothing to do but wait.

8 THE BENDS

1995 BEGAN WITH A BANG.

'High and Dry', which would prove to be the second single from the as yet unreleased second album, stormed into the Top Twenty. Better still, with the guitars aggressive yet deeply melodic and Yorke's vocal soaring, plummeting and pitch perfect, it provided conclusive evidence to suggest that Radiohead were finally to escape the grim, circling shadow of 'Creep'.

Radiohead played a few seriously low-key acoustic shows for their fans and then generously indulged Oxford Apollo with a homecoming performance of quite awesome emotional power (Awesome these days, like Terrible, is a hideously misused term. You can use it to describe Radiohead with no fear of contradiction). Present at the gig were some seventy journalists, who'd flown in from all around the globe on the strength of advance tapes of the album - as it turned out to be titled 'The Bends'. Also there were what appeared to be every single employee of EMI UK (the parent company of Parlophone), each of them presumably hoping to catch a glimpse of what the hell they were getting themselves into.

After the gig, back at the famously luxuriant Randolf Hotel, the band were their usual courteous selves, despite seeming a little strained by the presence of so many industry types. Yorke, unfortunately for him always the focal point for whichever beady eyes are about at the time, looked positively hounded. It was unsurprising, considering what, that very afternoon, he'd named as his major present concerns, the subjects that provided the lyrics to 'My Iron Lung' and much of the rest of 'The Bends', an album purposefully named after the potentially fatal pressure changes in the bloodstream when a diver rises too quickly from deep water to air.

"We were in New Zealand. We were taken to one of the most beautiful places I've ever seen in my life, the place where they filmed 'The Piano', and there I was, thinking 'This is wonderful. I don't think I've ever seen scenery so spectacular'. And suddenly it occurred to me that the only reason we were there was because... I can't put my finger on it, but something to do with the industry. a lot to do with MTV. And whenever you see MTV, there is a Coca-Cola machine right next to it. And I just felt like we were a part of it all. And all at once, the view lost all meaning."

Yorke also had a further, more specific complaint. 'The Bends' was to receive a simultaneous worldwide release, a state of affairs reserved only for records of the highest priority. 'Fake Plastic Trees' was marked down as a more than suitable single to be taken from it. But, in America something had happened.

"We're releasing 'Fake Plastic Trees' in America,' said Yorke 'and Capitol have remixed it. But it isn't as good as the original. The record company want us to release the remix, because they say it would suit American radio better. But that's a line we can't cross. I mean, it's a beautiful song as it stands. If it doesn't get on the radio the way it is now, then I don't think it's going to get on the radio at all. There's nothing anyone can do to it. And that really scares the shit out of me. I mean, if there's one reason why I'd give up this business, it's because people will try to fuck with your stuff to fit a formula. People say it won't work on the radio, but I have no fucking idea what they mean."

"The problem is, people are so fucking anxious now. They're worried by the idea that we might always stay The Band Who Did 'Creep'. And when things get like that, they can get seriously out of control. It's very weird. Very scary."

Early 1995 was a very strange time. With Kurt Cobain dead and Richey Edwards of the Manic Street Preachers inexplicably missing (actually there were a fair few likely explanations, but no one liked to countenance any of them. Still don't), people had begun to talk about a Culture Of Despair. After punk and the Slacker thing, there was an idea that there was an entire generation of people with no heroes, no prospects, no faith in government or religion. Deafened and poisoned by corporate lies and pollution, they watched helplessly as the world was systematically deprived of any means of natural regeneration (bad news for all but cockroaches and the super-rich). They had no real reason to stay alive. Yorke's lyrics, from 'Prove Yourself' onwards, seemed to place him firmly in this camp.

At the end of 1994, Yorke had said 'I'm sure there is a zeitgeist. There must be. You could see it happen with the Manics for a while. And I suppose for the past two years there was nothing we could have written about either... The stuff we've been going through is mind-altering. Emotionally and things. That sounds really over-dramatic, like we're playing up to it, but we're not really.'

In The Randolf, Yorke was clearer.

'I love life. I really do. But there's so much shit to deal with. Like, I have friends who are artists. Maybe even great artists. But they're at the end of their tethers. What with the dole, the poverty, they just don't have the energy to carry on. When we started this thing, I really did believe 'The Good will out, the Best rise to the top'. But I no longer believe that. People are continuously overlooked and ignored. You only have to watch the news to know that. It's not just artists. It's everybody.'

In March, 'The Bends' was finally released to almost unanimous critical acclaim, a fact that will certainly fail to amaze anyone who's heard it. Literally packed with top tunes, it was a far tighter offering than 'Pablo Honey'. With 'Bones' almost like Seventies glam, 'Sulk' jazzy as well as soaring and 'Just (Do It To Yourself)' a kind of frenzied anglo-grunge, it was also infinitely more varied, though still graced by the requisite number of classic Radiohead anthems - 'The Bends', 'High & Dry' and 'Fake Plastic Trees' - and heart-crushing ballads like 'Nice Dream'. It was a brilliant, brilliant album and, though it didn't immediately rival the million-selling 'Pablo Honey', it would certainly be legitimised by the longevity of its sales

But first there was another World Tour to enjoy and endure. Once again Radiohead were scheduled to go everywhere, including the UK where they headlined one day at the week-long Sound City Festival, this year situated in Bristol. Unfortunately, Yorke succumbing to gastric flu meant the last minute cancellation of a show in Sheffield, with Radiohead's management having to hand out teeshirts and open a free bar in order to prevent mortally disappointed fans from engaging in an impromptu riot. In April a Radiohead fan magazine called 'Answerphone' was launched, the first issue including a metal badge and poster for those who just couldn't get enough.

Then, with 'Fake Plastic Trees' a UK Top Twenty hit in May, it was off once more to Japan and the USA where, maybe because of that dodgy remix, the band found themselves far from the flavour of the month. The good news was that they had secured a support slot with REM for their all-dayer at Milton Keynes (capacity 130,000), along with Sleeper and The Cranberries, as well as a place on their tour to promote the 'Monster' LP in Europe and America. Milton Keynes sent 'The Bends' rocketing back into the UK charts - it would eventually go platinum.

The REM tour was a positive joy for Radiohead, not least because they'd been hardcore fans for years. They'd even, as On A Friday, occasionally been compared. Although extremely nervous to begin with, they soon settled into the rhythm of things, partially because, in Berlin on the second night of the tour, both bands had got catastrophically drunk at a record company party **featuring enormous inflatable dinosaurs.**

From then on the two groups got along famously. Yorke was profoundly impressed by the way Michael Stipe coped with a level of fame most major stars only dream of (dignity appeared to be the key) and also by a message bassist Mike Mills had received from President Clinton enquiring after the state of his stomach. All of Radiohead were wholly taken by the way REM would write songs on the road, run through a perfunctory rehearsal during soundcheck and then have the unmitigated bottle to slip them into the set later that night. This clearly was what real bands can do. They were also understandably elated when Stipe announced onstage in Tel Aviv that

'There aren't many things that scare me, bu

In August, having supported Neil Young in Denmark, Radiohead released a fourth single from 'The Bends', this time 'Just', yet another Top Twenty hit. A pattern was quite obviously beginning to emerge. Radiohead, despite Yorke's lifelong problems with his own self-image, were undeniably impressing vast throngs of people with their videos. And who'd argue with 'High & Dry' where the band are shot through a radar screen, playing against a juggernaut in the pouring rain. Or 'Fake Plastic Trees' where Yorke is crushed into a shopping trolley and wheeled around a surreal and not altogether wholesome supermarket. Or the extraordinary 'Just' where a man lies down on the pavement and refuses to rise, much to the consternation of passers-by. Radiohead bang out their song in a room nearby as the pedestrians finally get the man to give his reasons and, having heard them, all lie down beside him. That's classic Radiohead, an ambivalent study in stubbornness, hopelessness and reason.

Throughout the year, the band's songs persistently wound up on soundtracks and compilations. 'Fake Plastic Trees' turned up in Alicia Silverstone's 'Clueless', 'High & Dry' formed part of Polygram TV's 'Acoustic Rock' package and the band also contributed to the 'Rocks Off' compilation (along with Oasis and Guns N' Roses) and the soundtrack to the snowboarding video 'Odd Man Out' (with Leftfield, Jamiroquai and, again Oasis). More importantly, they also spent two days writing and recording a track called 'Lucky' for the 'Help' album. This LP proved a miracle of organisation as such luminaries as Noel Gallagher, Paul Weller, Paul McCartney, The Charlatans and The Chemical Brothers all successfully put together tracks within a ridiculously short space of time, the project eventually netting millions for the children of Bosnia. 'Lucky' was the song chosen to front the first 'Help' EP, a single that also included a bulldozing live version of PJ.Harvey's '50ft Queenie'. Strangely, despite the charity-work involved, 'Lucky' was not granted daytime airplay. Perhaps if Thom Yorke had worn a red nose... no, perhaps not.

adiohead are so good they scare me'.

On a more personal note, the concept of less than fair play reared its ugly head again when it came to the announcement of the nominees for the Mercury Prize. Despite their lukewarm response to 'My Iron Lung' most publications were fast coming around to idea that 'The Bends' was facing little competition in the Album Of The Year stakes. For the Mercury Prize however, Radiohead made it into the last twelve but not the final shortlist of ten. Even those who find awards for artistic achievement inherently foolish were shocked and the eventual winners, Portishead, whose 'Dummy' LP was indubitably a masterpiece of trip-hop soul, graciously confirmed everyone's suspicions when they said that Radiohead should have triumphed in their place.

No worries. Radiohead took off back to the States to support Dave Pirner and Soul Asylum whose 'Let Your Dim Light Shine' album had proved a disastrous follow-up to the multi-million-selling 'Grave Dancers Union'. Radiohead's relatively minor Stateside problems with 'The Bends' were well and truly shaded. And though the two bands might at first have seemed to have little, well, nothing in common, Soul Asylum had spent the best part of a decade struggling to survive, both as non-entities and major label victims and Pirner had, during one terrible period, been sent to the edge of insanity by tinnitus. They're also a hell of a laugh, more than capable of matching Radiohead's grim seriousness and vibrant good nature. To the amazement of many, they got on great, the only downpoint being when Radiohead had all the gear stolen at a gig in Canada (after the Tears For Fears experience it's a wonder they went back at all).

The year ended with a Winter tour of the UK, beginning at Glasgow's Barrowlands and culminating at Brixton Academy. 'The Bends' was recognised almost right across the board as the Album Of The Year and the gigs were righteously celebratory, one review enthusing 'See the sweat, drown in the howls and gasp at the love-sick eyes of 2,000 people who pogo out of their socks at the joy of seeing Radiohead back. and that's just to the slow, depressing numbers.' Some Euro dates sold out too, a rare occurrence in 1995, though there were rumours that Thom Yorke had lost his voice during a concert in Munich and fled the stage in tears with the band having only performed five songs.

If that was the peak of his worries then 1995 had turned out to be a good one after all.

9 STREET SPIRIT

THE BEGINNING OF 1996 SAW RADIOHEAD TAKE THEIR PLACE AT THE VERY TOP OF BRITISH MUSIC With their confidence finally expanded by years of ups and downs and even more ups, and their worldview modified by touring with the been-there, seen-that likes of Michael Stipe and Dave Pirner they finally allowed themselves the luxury of a holiday and, while they were away, once more with no press or radio play, 'Street Spirit' (yet another single from 'The Bends') became their biggest hit to date. 'The Bends' itself returned to the charts, entering the Top Ten - something it hadn't actually done when first released.

Nominated for Best Album, Best Video and Best Band at The Brits (all categories won by by Oasis - shock, horror), Thom Yorke, along with Brian Eno collected the Freddie Mercury Award on behalf of all the artists who had participated in the making of the 'Help' album. The band also involved themselves in the Rock The Vote campaign, as modelled on the American version which, aided by the likes of Eddie Vedder, REM and Madonna, was widely cited as one of the factors contributing to Bill Clinton's victory over the Republicans at the last Presidential election. Radiohead's move in this direction was explained to Melody Maker by Ed O'Brien who said that the band had been heavily influenced by REM's habit of taking ten organisations out on the road with them (one being Rock The Vote) and allowing them to set up stalls at their gigs. He also mentioned that Radiohead had just leased their own rehearsal space, an old apple shed they'd converted, and were working on new material. They were hoping, he said, to take a leaf out of the Beastie Boys' book, get their own recording equipment in a very low-key rehearsal room, and record things when they were fresh and exciting.

Back from holiday, the band once more toured across Canada, Europe and the USA. One Canadian date, their biggest yet, headlining before 5,000 people was said to have seen Thom Yorke in his best mood for years, an upbeat and truly confident version of his former tortured self. Their headlining performance at Glasgow's T In The Park was proof positive. Radiohead are here to stay. Because they LOVE it.

10 TALK RADIO

AN INTERVIEW WITH THOM YORKE FOLLOWING RADIOHEAD'S SHOWCASE CONCERT IN NEW YORK, JUNE 1996.

So how are you feeling?

We just wanna go home. It's been a difficult few weeks. But, at the same time, we're quite elated really. It's stimulating. It's been a period of big ups and downs and a real test of our convictions.

What have been the low points?

Being ill and being nice to people really. I'm not very good at that. If people give me enough booze, I'm usually all right.

You must be keen to push the LP as far as it will go here.

The temptation there is just to keep going, but that would be at the expense of whatever might happen when we stopped. All you're doing is prolonging the eventual... comedown or shipwreck. I'd like to have a life really. We did a similar thing with the first album, toured until we were complete vegetables. There's no point in doing that again, the damage would be obvious.

But surely the band is your life, touring is your life. you don't need another.

That's not true because what the fuck are you gonna write about?

You see life, you meet people, you could write hotel-room songs. the sense of alienation would be the same.

Being a touring band and being good at it is not everything to me. It's a job, you know? I'm much more into the idea of recording. I admire Oasis for sticking to it, but we did that with 'Creep' and in the end it did us nothing but damage. It took us a good year and a half to get where we are now, to be able to emotionally cope with it. We're wimps basically... The thing that kept us going was the elation of people's responses, then it's not difficult going out and enjoying it and listening to each other play. But then the work sort of exploded and everything opened up. we started writing a lot more and it started making more sense. There wasn't this Everything's Gonna Fall Apart feeling all the time. That's why it's important for us to go with that.

The fear of not amounting to anything was a factor then.

Yeah, and I don't have that anymore. It's been embarrassingly well-received. We could really start loving it. the best thing to do is to stay quiet, especially back home. I'm not really into people coming round to my house, knocking on my door, just to look at me.

You sound much more confident than you were before.

I just feel more confident about my work. and I think we have the confidence not to tear each other apart and tear everything we do apart before we've even done it, which is what used to happen. then you go into paroxysms of fear and self-loathing and everything gets very boring. I don't think I've particularly lightened up or anything, but I know I have found a path I wanna go down. It's very uplifting for me. That's why I'm trying to avoid the press. The confidence side is so important to me because I'm not a particularly confident person. I just don't want to expose us to it because it could destroy us.

Are you suspicious of the press?

I don't read any of that stuff and, besides, I don't think my life is intriguing enough and what we do doesn't interest them enough. we're not a pop band in the same way that Pulp are. I'm not going to do talk shows, I'm not a personality.

Do you think you have an affinity in this with Michael Stipe?

I admire the way he dealt with that whole period of his life around 'Automatic For The People', with the AIDS rumours. He just wasn't gonna answer and they did give up eventually. Elvis Costello was the same. He just walked away from it all. If you love it so much then you're asking for trouble.

Don't you see the commercial appeal of the talk show thing?

I can't. Radiohead are just not into that talk show mindset, wanting to be personalities. We're no good at it. The most important thing in our lives is trying to maintain enough control for us to carry on being creative.

Your last tour was pretty massive. Why would anyone want to get to that level?

I didn't before but, having seen U2 and REM, there is still something you can offer in that situation. You just have to rewrite the way you feel about it. The thing that worries me more than anything else is making a record that lives up to all this hype. We've only just learnt to do this. REM and U2 and Costello have been around a lot longer. And I think it's a dangerous thing to be locked 100% into the mentality where we can be that sort of band.

How is the writing going for the next album?

I'm writing a lot more on tour, but your mind is going round at a different speed so there's no way of judging it. You just take your notes and tapes home. That's the nature of any creative process. There's always that liberating thing of spending, say, a week on something and then throwing it away.

Do you think about how your fans might connect to it?

I'm just writing a lot of gibberish. It's sort of like a curse that people listen to my voice and think that everything I sing is important. I find it highly amusing. Same with Scott Walker. If you wrote the words down they'd sound really silly.

True. You can hear the words to 'Fake Plastic Trees' very clearly, but still have no idea what they're about.

Yeah, me too. For me it wasn't about any of the words that I wrote but about the melody. The words were treated very much as noise, except perhaps the last verse which means something to me. The rest is gibberish, not relevant.

How do you feel about that burn-out idea, where you become a moth pushed into the flames?

I sort of thought that was happening last year. That gig in Germany, named 'Thom's temper tantrum' by the NME, I was supposed to have gone off in a huff. In actual fact I'd been ill. This quack doctor gave me all these drugs and told me I'd be fine. I did freak out but everyone was really supportive. I don't think people have any interest in me

personally burning myself up. And, for myself, I'm very anti the whole emoting thing, you know. I just have my eyes shut, don't move or do anything. I'm not driven all the time, I can't possibly be driven all the time, and it feels really good to just stand there, just walk up and look out the front.

Thinking about the Culture Of Despair, do you ever wonder if you might be a bad influence on some people?

Any artist who worries about their audience and how their audience is going to react is stuffed. Yeah, people accuse us of being maudlin and depressing and so on, but the people who come to the shows get the point that it's not about that, it's about the music transcending how depressed I was when I wrote it. But to the parents, yeah, it's like Joy Division.

Do you get difficult letters from fans?

I don't actually get many letters like that at all. I'm quite surprised. It happened around the 'Creep' thing because of what was projected around it, none of which was our responsibility. That was what they picked up on. The letters aren't exactly funnels of joy.

Do you ever feel isolated? It must be strange being cosseted, driven in limos from hotels to airports to hotels.

I always feel like that when I go to LA. People generally get the message that we don't want to be looked after, but that's probably me kidding myself. I get more disturbed by the idea that I'm moving round the world so fast and everything is going by like flashes before your eye. You know that point where you're about to die, where your whole life is flashing before your eyes? I seem to get that a lot.

What's your worst fear for the band?

Making a crap record.

Turning into a bad stadium act might be worse.

I don't think that's in us. I'd much rather stay at home and do an album at the bottom of the garden and not tour. Like Tom Waits.

But isn't it all part of the process. You stay in big hotels, you play in huge stadiums, you get complacent...

That's why the most important thing in my life at the moment is establishing something outside of this. It's almost like a frantic desperation thing. At Christmas I tried to do it by shopping, by spending money on household appliances, taking them home and presenting them to my girlfriend and the other girl who lives in the house and saying 'Here you go'. The house is scattered with stuff, in boxes mostly, that I bought to try and claim my life back.

Does it feel weird being recognised in shops?

I'm a compulsive shopper anyway. Oxford's good for that, they don't really bother you. I don't think I'm seen as a particularly approachable person even by Radiohead fans. I've got that sort of face. This guy two days ago came up and said 'Hey! You're that guy from Radiohead' and I didn't sort of say anything and he went 'Hey! You're a rude fucker'. At home I really enjoy denying who I am, I do it on a regular basis. The look of confusion on people's faces is nice. I do seem to expend a lot of energy and time trying to avoid the issue when I get home.

What about the next album?

I have every intention of the next record being a grateful record. I don't give a fuck, it won't be in any way less valid. It will be a grateful record. I could fall into the trap of thinking 'Oh my God, I've got to supply another maudlin one' but the way that we're writing and the way that it's happening and the way that we feel when we play together is about release and it's grateful and it'll hopefully be good because of that. We're not trying to prove anything and I think that's a good thing for Radiohead.

Thanks to Jim Shelly and Ben Mothersole.

dumb